SONGS OF
Stephen Foster
FOR THE
UKULELE

ARRANGED BY

DICK SHERIDAN

View of the Upper Mississippi
Ferdinand Richardt - 1865

Design & Typography by Roy "Rick" Dains

ISBN 978-1-57424-316-1

Grateful acknowledgment is given for the assistance of the Foster Hall Collection, Center for American Music, University of Pittsburgh Library System. The Center for American Music is an archive, a research center, and a public museum dedicated to American music, with a focus on Stephen Foster.

Copyright ©2015 CENTERSTREAM Publishing, LLC
P. O. Box 17878 - Anaheim Hills, CA 92817
email: centerstream@aol.com • web: centerstream-usa.com

INTRODUCTION

No music is dearer to the American heart than that of Stephen Foster. His glorious, immortal melodies have stood the test of time, many of which are as popular today as they were 150 years ago. Considered to be America's first professional songwriter, Foster composed nearly 200 works, an amazing accomplishment for his brief life span of only 37 years. His vast array of enduring favorites ranged from sentimental love songs to poignant parlor favorites and lively numbers from the blackface minstrel stage. How depleted our treasury of popular music would be without his "Oh! Susanna," "Camptown Races," "Beautiful Dreamer," and "Jeanie With The Light Brown Hair."

Foster's first success came in 1848 with the publishing of "Oh! Susanna" and "Uncle Ned." He received $100 for these songs, but because of limited copyright protection, other publishers printed their own versions and realized thousands without paying royalties.

In 1849 Foster entered into an exclusive publishing arrangement with Firth, Pond & Co., a relationship that lasted until 1860 and encompassed his most productive years. Blackface minstrelsy was enormously popular during this period and Foster began writing almost totally for this form of entertainment. Following sale of his song "Old Folks At Home" to E.P. Christy, founder of the famous Christy Minstrels, an agreement was made to have the well-known troupe introduce his songs in exchange for sheet music credit of "As sung by the Christy Minstrels."

The popularity of blackface "Ethiopian" minstrelsy at the time cannot be over estimated. Foster's songs were written when slavery was in force and black dialect was popular with minstrel groups. Sadly, many of the songs and routines were unquestionably racist with trashy lyrics and satirical situations. This was offensive to Foster who felt great compassion and affection for those sadly in bondage to slavery. He endeavored to "build up taste" by writing lyrics that respected the speech and ennobled the life of plantation slaves. Although many of his lyrics were in black dialect they were not mocking. In fact he instructed minstrel singers to perform his songs with dignity and instructed publishers not to include degrading caricatures on sheet music covers and broadsides.

In deference to the sensibilities of some readers, several of the original words of Foster's songs have been changed in this collection. However, to be true to the times when these songs were written, there is one exception, "Massa's In The Cold Ground." It is hoped that you will concur that this song shows only sincere sentiment and no disrespect. It must be remembered that when slavery was in practice many of the slaves were not long separated from their native land and language. Foster was sensitive to their speech and tried to duplicate it with warmth and understanding. In another song, "Old Black Joe," although the lyrics are not in dialect, this same sensitivity applies and the song is in no way demeaning.

Despite so many of Foster's song being linked with plantation life and the South, he had visited the South only once on a steamboat honeymoon trip to New Orleans. Most of his productive years were spent in Pittsburgh, eventually moving to New Jersey and New York City where he could be closer to publishers.

During his lifetime Foster did receive royalties, in amounts in today's dollars that would reach millions. Although his works achieved great popularity, Foster himself was relatively unknown; he never performed his songs professionally. But fame and fortune can be elusive, and with the raging of the Civil War and his reduced productivity and waning interest by publishers, Foster fell on hard times. His debts increased and he was reduced to selling rights to future songs and for advanced royalties for songs that were never produced. Separated from his wife and daughter, he drifted into alcoholism, loneliness, and despair. His final years in New York City were spent in lodging houses, hotels, and a saloon in the back of a neighborhood grocery store. Despite shabby clothes and being reduced to selling a few songs for cash in hand and the price of a drink, he never appeared intoxicated and was always thought to be a gentleman – courteous and well mannered.

It is pitifully sad that the life of Stephen Foster should have ended so tragically. Yet his legacy of music lives on, from early minstrel days, through vaudeville, and on into the repertoires of classical divas, parlor performers, folk singers, and bluegrass bands. Indeed, his beautiful songs remain fresh as new and are truly immortal.

STEPHEN COLLINS FOSTER
1826 - 1864

TABLE OF CONTENTS

BEAUTIFUL DREAMER

Ukulele tuning: gCEA

STEPHEN C. FOSTER

1.Beau-ti-ful Dream-er, wake un-to me, star-light and dew-drop are wait-ing for

thee. _____ Sounds of the rude world heard in the day,

lull'd by the moon-light have all pass'd a - way. _____

Beau-ti-ful Dream-er, queen of my song, ___ list while I woo thee with soft mel-o-dy.

BEAUTIFUL DREAMER

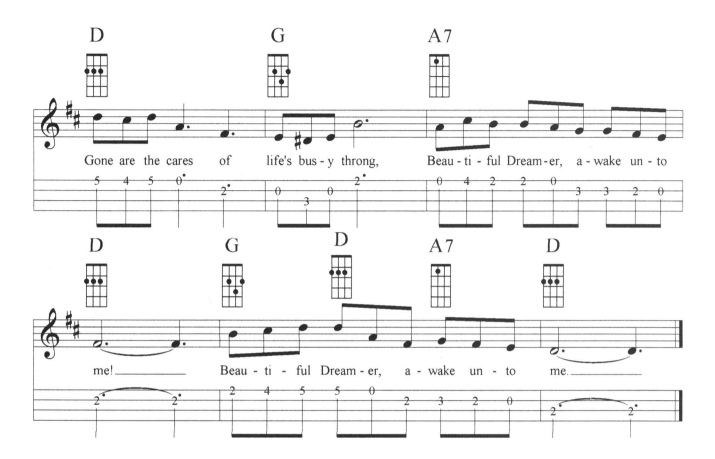

Gone are the cares of life's bus-y throng, Beau-ti-ful Dream-er, a-wake un-to me! Beau-ti-ful Dream-er, a-wake un-to me.

2. Beautiful Dreamer, out on the sea,
    Mermaids are chanting their wild Lorelei.
    Over the streamlet vapors are borne,
    Waiting to fade at the bright coming morn.

Beautiful Dreamer, beam on my heart,
E'en as the moon on the streamlet and sea;
Then will all clouds of sorrow depart,
Beautiful Dreamer, awake unto me!
Beautiful Dreamer, awake unto me!

Dolce far Niente
John William Waterhouse - 1880

THE CAMPTOWN RACES

Ukulele tuning: gCEA

STEPHEN C. FOSTER

THE CAMPTOWN RACES

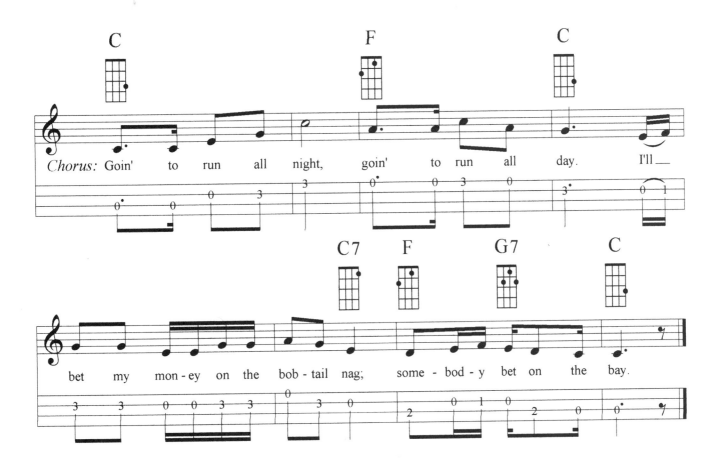

Chorus: Goin' to run all night, goin' to run all day. I'll

bet my mon-ey on the bob-tail nag; some-bod-y bet on the bay.

2. The long-tail filly and the big black horse,
   Doo-dah! Doo-dah!
   They fly the track and they both cut across,
   Oh! Doo-dah-day!
   The blind horse sinking in a big mud hole,
   Doo-dah! Doo-dah!
   Can't touch bottom with a ten foot pole,
   Oh! Doo-dah-day!

3. Old muley cow comes onto the track,
   Doo-dah! Doo-dah!
   The bobtail flung her over his back,
   Oh! Doo-dah-day!

   Then fly along like a railroad car,
   Doo-dah! Doo-dah!
   Running a race with a shootin' star,
   Oh! Doo-dah-day!

4. See them flying on a ten-mile heat,
   Doo-dah! Doo-dah!
   'Round the racetrack then repeat,
   Oh! Doo-dah-day!
   I win my money on the bobtail nag,
   Doo-dah! Doo-dah!
   I keep my money in an old tow bag,
   Oh! Doo-dah-day!

Detail from poster for *Christy's Minstrels* - circa 1840s

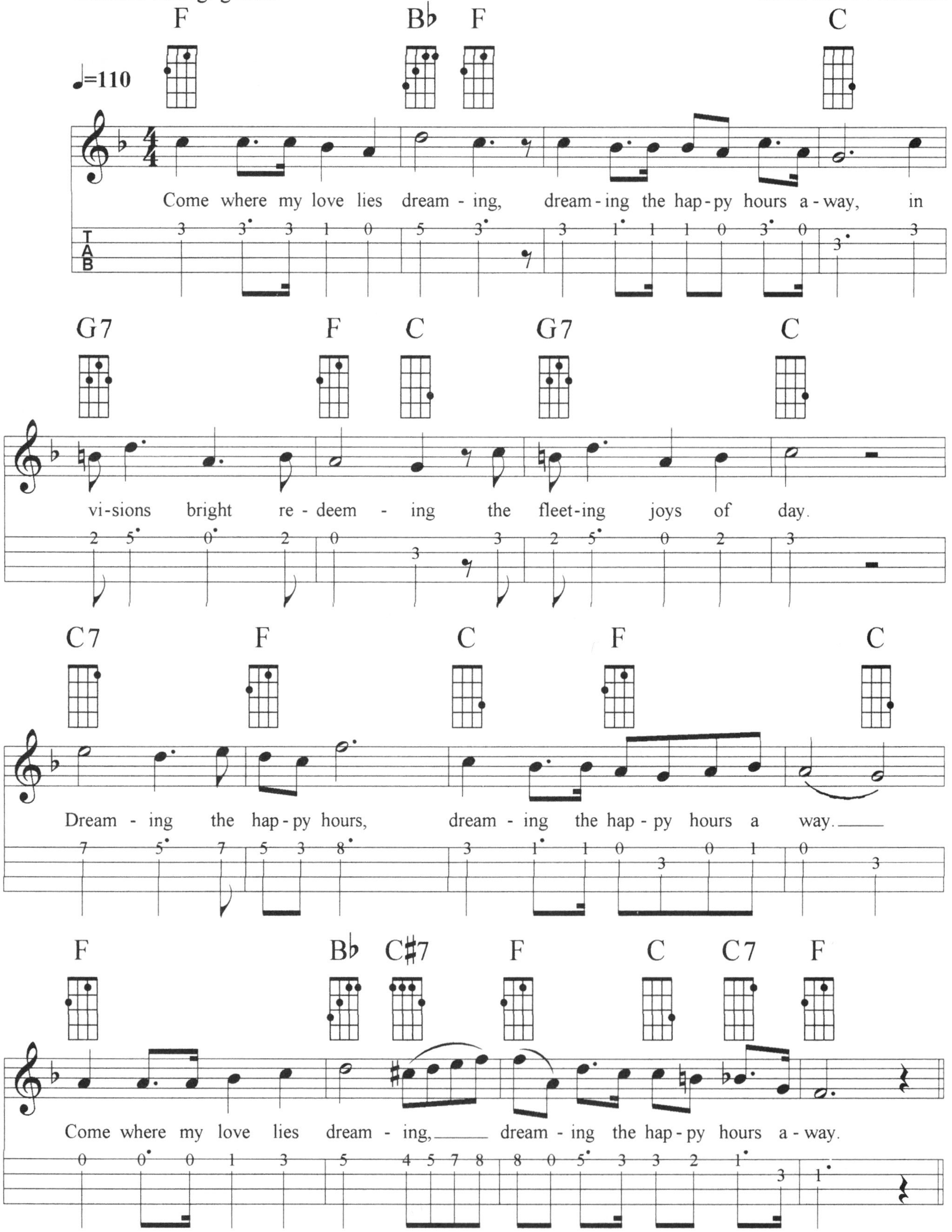

Come Where My Love Lies Dreaming

Ukulele tuning: gCEA

STEPHEN FOSTER

F Bb F C
=110
Come where my love lies dream - ing, dream - ing the hap - py hours a - way, in
G7 F C G7 C
vi - sions bright re - deem - ing the fleet - ing joys of day.
C7 F C F C
Dream - ing the hap - py hours, dream - ing the hap - py hours a way.
F Bb C#7 F C C7 F
Come where my love lies dream - ing, dream - ing the hap - py hours a - way.

COME WHERE MY LOVE LIES DREAMING

It was a poignant conclusion to Stephen Foster's young life when mourners reached the cemetery following the funeral at Pittsburgh's Trinity Church. As his remains were lowered into the grave a brass band was heard to play the gentle but plaintive strains of "Come Where My Love Lies Dreaming." Although many monuments and memorials have since been dedicated, Stephen was buried beneath a simple headstone ineloquently marking the final resting place of this gifted soul:

STEPHEN C. FOSTER
of Pittsburgh, PA
Born July 4, 1826
Died January 13, 1864

Among the Sierra Nevada Mountains
Albert Bierstadt - 1868

THE GLENDY BURK

Ukulele tuning: gCEA

STEPHEN C. FOSTER

THE GLENDY BURK

2. The Glendy Burk has a funny old crew
      And they sing the boatman's song,
   They burn the pitch and the pine knot too,
      For to shove the boat along.
   The smoke goes up and the engine roars,
      And the wheel goes 'round and 'round,
   So fare you well! I'll take a little ride
      When the Glendy Burk comes down.
   CHORUS

3. I'll work all night in the wind and storm,
      I'll work all day in the rain,
   'Til I find myself on the levy dock
      In New Orleans again.
   They make me mow in the hayfield here
      And knock my head with the flail,
   I'll go where they work with the sugar and the cane
      And roll on the cotton bale.
   CHORUS

4. My lady love is pretty as a peach,
      I'll meet her on the way,
   I'll take her back to the sunny old south,
      And there I'll make her stay.
   So don't you fret my honey dear,
      Oh! Don't you fret Miss Brown,
   I'll take you back 'fore the middle of the week
      When the Glendy Burk comes down.
   CHORUS

Steamboat Delta Queen
Circa 1920s

Every several years or so there's a festival in Cincinnati on the Ohio River called Tall Stacks. Paddle wheelers come from all over the Mississippi river to the Ohio, from as far north as Michigan and up from New Orleans and the deep south. I've had the goodfortune to play for the event several times aboard the authentic steamboat, the "Belle of Louisville." The "Belle" is one of the larger ships like the "Delta Queen," the "Mississippi Queen" and the enormous "American Queen." But there are much smaller boats too, and the river and docks are dotted with a variety of many sizes.

In addition to the music that I was part of creating in the grand salon of the "Belle," there was the sound of steam calliopes echoing off the hills together with horn toots from ships coming and going. The calliope's shrill notes could be heard for miles, a traditionally way of alerting towns along the river of the boat's arrival. And for those special riverboats that provided entertainment, the calliope served to draw in the crowds and evoke the excited cries on shore of "Here comes the showboat!"

Stephen Foster tunes have always been standard fare for the calliope. Lively songs like "Oh! Susanna" and "The Camptown Races" set the mood for fun and gaiety, while "My Old Kentucky Home" celebrates with nostalgic sentiment the state right across the river from Cincinnati.

The "hurricane roof" mentioned in "The Glendy Burk" is the topmost deck of the boat, sometimes enclosed and sometimes not, providing passengers with an unobstructed view of passing scenery — and the ship's captain with a good vantage point for navigation — and for checking up on the crew.

Hard Times
Come Again No More

Ukulele tuning: gCEA

STEPHEN C. FOSTER

1.Let us pause in life's plea-sures and count its man-y tears while we

all sup sor-row with the poor. There's a song that will lin-ger for-

ev-er in our ears; Oh! hard times, come a-gain no more. *Chorus:* 'Tis the

song, the sigh of the wea-ry; hard times, hard times,

HARD TIMES

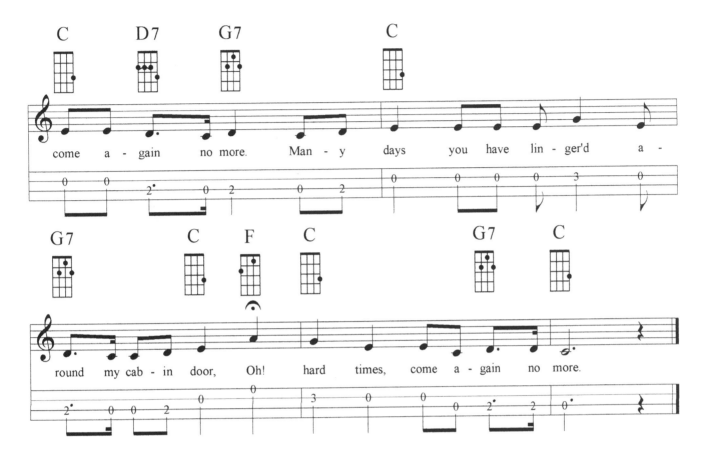

come a - gain no more. Man - y days you have lin - ger'd a -

round my cab - in door, Oh! hard times, come a - gain no more.

2. While we seek mirth and beauty
      and music light and gay,
   There are frail forms fainting at the door.

   Though their voices are silent,
      their pleading looks will say,
   Oh! Hard Times Come Again No More.
   CHORUS

Surprisingly, for a song written over 150 years ago, "Hard Times" still has a relevancy today. Contemporary performers like Emmylou Harris, Bob Dylan, Johnny Cash and Bruce Springsteen have picked up on its haunting melody and troubling message.

Indeed, for Foster himself, hard times did come. Estranged from his wife and family, and with only limited earnings from his music, he died in penury at the age of 37 in a New York City hospital. Sadly, he had become alcoholic, selling his songs for the price of a drink. At the time of his death, the sum of his assets was three pennies and 38 cents in Civil War script.

Jeanie with the Light Brown Hair

Ukulele tuning: gCEA

STEPHEN C. FOSTER

I dream of Jean-ie with the light brown hair, borne like a va-por

on the sum-mer air; I see her trip-ping where the bright streams play,

hap-py as the dai-sies that dance on her way.

Man-y were the wild notes her mer-ry voice would pour,

JEANIE WITH THE LIGHT BROWN HAIR

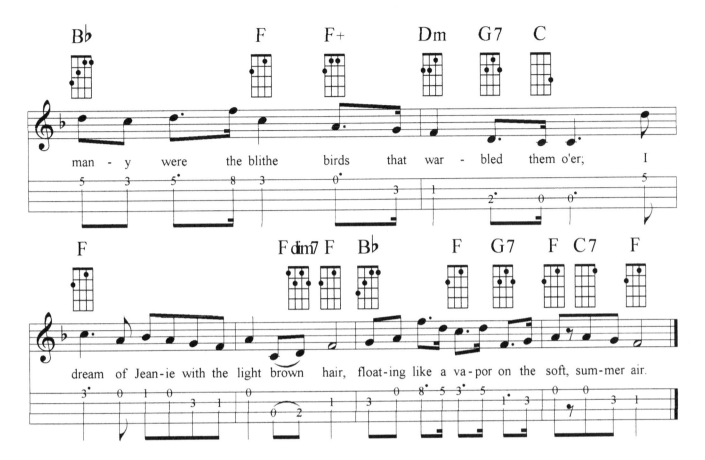

man - y were the blithe birds that war - bled them o'er; I

dream of Jean-ie with the light brown hair, float-ing like a va-por on the soft, sum-mer air.

I sigh for Jeanie, but her light form strayed,
 Far from the fond hearts 'round her native glade;
Her smiles have vanished and her sweet songs flown,
 Flitting like the dreams that have cheered us and gone.

Now the nodding willd flow'rs may wither on the shore,
 Where her gentle fingers will cull them no more;
I sigh for Jeanie with the light brown hair,
 Floating like a vapor on the soft, summer air.

Separated from his wife, Jane and daughter,
Marion after only three years of marriage, Foster
was living in New York City when he wrote this
song for his wife in 1854.

AT RIGHT:
Unidentified Woman, Circa 1850
Photographer Unknown

Massa's in De Cold Ground

Ukulele tuning: gCEA

STEPHEN C. FOSTER

MASSA'S IN DE COLD GROUND

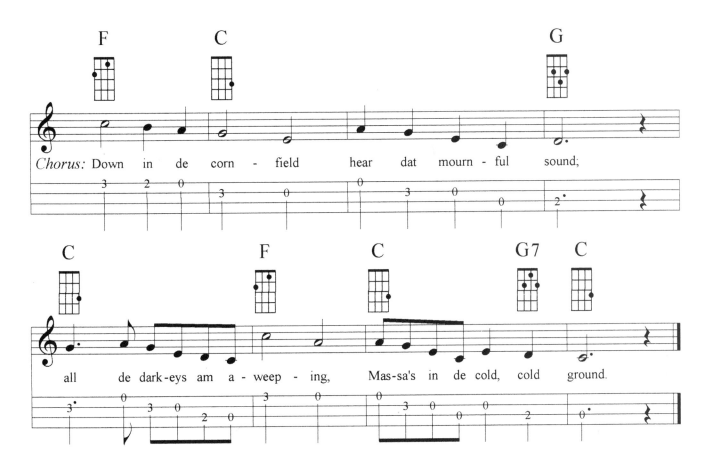

Chorus: Down in de corn - field hear dat mourn - ful sound;

all de dark-eys am a - weep - ing, Mas-sa's in de cold, cold ground.

2. When de autumn leaves were falling,
    when de days were cold,
'Twas hard to hear old Massa calling,
    cayse he was so weak and old.
Now de orange trees am blooming,
    on de sandy shore,
Now de summer days am coming,
    Massa nebber calls no more.
CHORUS

3. Massa make de darkeys love him,
    cayse he was so kind,
Now day sadly weep above him,
    mourning cayse he leave dem behind.
I cannot work before tomorrow,
    cayse de tear drop flow,
I try to drive away my sorrow,
    pickin' on de old banjo.
CHORUS

Picking Cotton
Ballou's Pictorial - 1858

My Old Kentucky Home, Good Night

Ukulele tuning: gCEA

STEPHEN C. FOSTER

1. The sun shines bright in my old Ken-tuck-y home, t'is sum-mer, the sea-son is
   young folks roll on the lit-tle cab-in floor, all mer-ry, all hap-py, and

gay; the corn top's ripe and the mead-ow's in the bloom, while the
bright; by'n by hard times come a-knock-ing at the door, then my ___

birds make mu-sic all the day. The Old Ken-tuck-y Home, good-night.

MY OLD KENTUCKY HOME, GOOD NIGHT

2. They hunt no more for the possum and the coon,
   on the meadow, the hill and the shore;
   They sing no more by the glimmer of the moon,
   on the bench by the old cabin door.
   The day goes by like a shadow o'er the heart,
   with sorrow where all was delight;
   The time has come when the families have to part,
   then my old Kentucky Home, good-night.
   CHORUS

3. The head must bow and the back will have to bend,
   wherever the darky may go,
   A few more days and the trouble will all end,
   in the field where the sugar canes grow.
   A few more days to tote the weary load,
   no matter 'twill never be light;
   A few more days till we totter on the road,
   then my Old Kentucky Home, good-night.
   CHORUS

NELLY BLY

Ukulele tuning: gCEA

STEPHEN C. FOSTER

NELLY BLY

2. Nelly Bly! Has a voice like the turtle dove,
  I hear it in the meadow
  and I hear it in the grove.

Nelly Bly has a heart warm as a cup of tea,
  and bigger than the sweet potato,
  down in Tennessee.
  CHORUS

23

23

NELLY WAS A LADY

Ukulele tuning: gCEA

STEPHEN C. FOSTER

Down on the Mis-sis-sip-i float - ing, long time I trav-el on the way;

all night the cot-ton wood a-tot - ing, sing for my true love all the day.

Refrain: Nel - ly was a la - dy, last night she died;

toll the bell for love-ly Nell, my dark Vir-gin-ny bride.

NELLY WAS A LADY

2. Now I'm unhappy and I'm weeping
   Can't tote the cottonwood no more;
   Last night when Nelly was a-sleeping,
   Death came a-knocking at the door.
   REFRAIN

3. When I saw my Nelly in the morning,
   Smiled 'till she opened up her eyes,
   Seemed like the light of day a-dawning,
   Just 'fore the sun begins to rise.
   REFRAIN

4. Close by the margin of the water,
   Where the lone weeping willow grows,
   There lived Virginia's lovely daughter;
   There she in death may find repose.
   REFRAIN

5. Down in the meadow 'mong the clover,
   Walk with my Nelly by my side;
   Now all the happy days are over,
   Farewell, my dear Virginny bride.
   REFRAIN

Grove of trees along the Mississippi

OH! SUSANNA

Ukulele tuning: gCEA

STEPHEN C. FOSTER

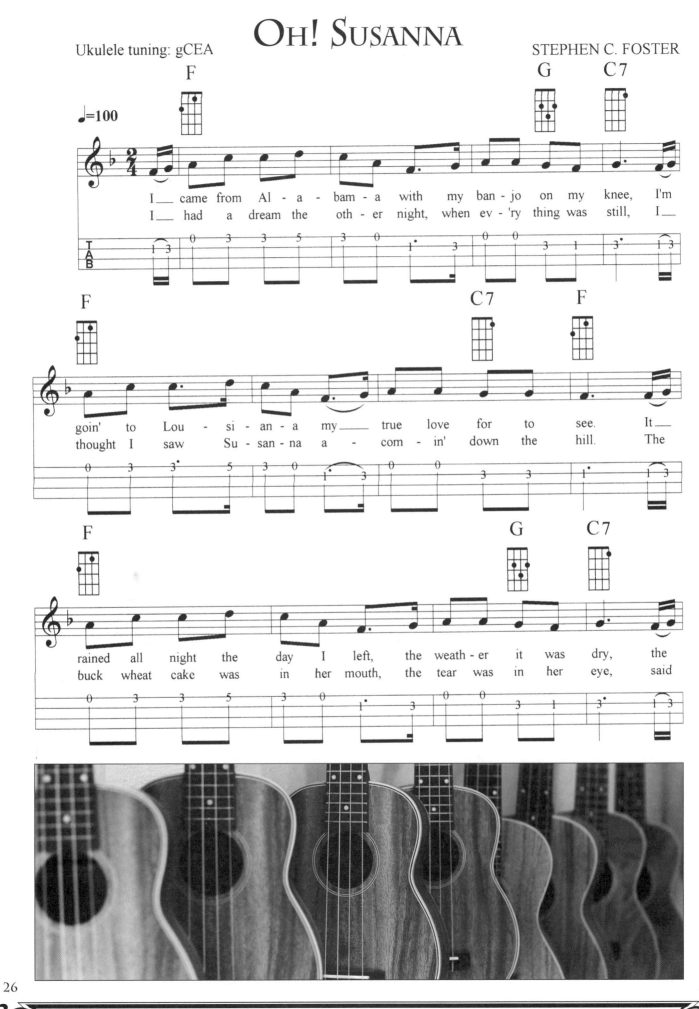

I __ came from Al - a - bam - a with my ban - jo on my knee, I'm
I __ had a dream the oth - er night, when ev - 'ry thing was still, I __

goin' to Lou - si - an - a my __ true love for to see. It __
thought I saw Su - san - na a - com - in' down the hill. The

rained all night the day I left, the weath - er it was dry, the
buck wheat cake was in her mouth, the tear was in her eye, said

OH! SUSANNA

I once was asked, "What's the name of that song they always play in the Old West movies, the one in the saloon scenes where there's a piano player wearing a striped shirt, arm garters, and a derby hat with a sign on the wall saying DON'T SHOOT THE PIANO PLAYER?" "Golden Slippers," I suggested. "No, no, not that one!" came the emphatic response. I tried again, How about "Turkey in the Straw?" Again, no luck. Then it dawned on me, "Oh! Susanna?" I asked. That time I struck paydirt, and it's no wonder. "Oh! Susanna" is one of America's best known songs and surely one of Foster's most popular.

Written in 1848, just at the time when the California Gold Rush was gaining momentum, the song became the unofficial anthem of prospecting "Forty-Niners" who came from Alabama and elsewhere with a "washpan" on their knee instead of a banjo. The song was written as a minstrel number with a lively polka beat that was popular at the time. Over 100,000 copies were eventually sold but allegedly Foster only received payment of $100. Because of uncertain copyright laws, many unscrupulous publishers printed the song without paying royalties.

OLD BLACK JOE

Ukulele tuning: gCEA

STEPHEN C. FOSTER

1.Gone are the days when my heart was young and gay; gone are my friends from the cot - ton fields a - way; gone from the earth to a bet - ter land I know, I hear their gen - tle voi - ces call - ing, "Old Black Joe!" I'm

Refrain

OLD BLACK JOE

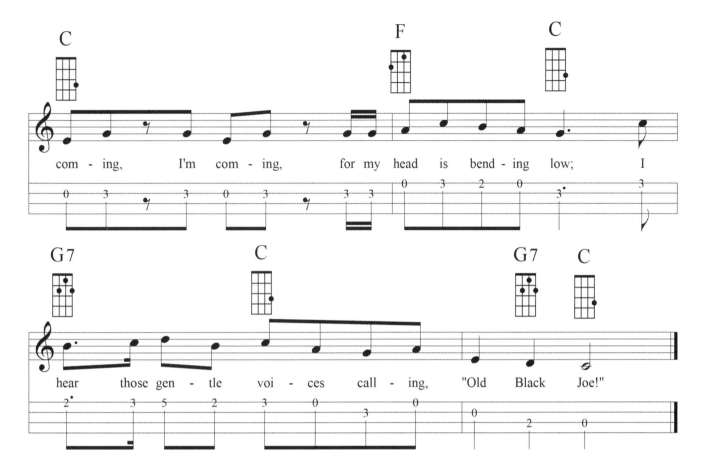

com - ing, I'm com - ing, for my head is bend - ing low; I

hear those gen - tle voi - ces call - ing, "Old Black Joe!"

2. Why do I weep when my heart
       should feel no pain?
    Why do I sigh that my friends
       come not again?
    Grieving for forms
       now departed long ago,
    I hear their gentle voices calling,
       "Old Black Joe!"
    REFRAIN

3. Where are the hearts
       once so happy and so free?
    The children so dear
       that I held upon my knee?
    Gone to the shore
       where my soul has longed to go,
    I hear their gentle voices calling,
       "Old Black Joe!"
    REFRAIN

AT LEFT:
Unidentified Banjo Player - 1930s
Photographer Unknown

OLD DOG TRAY

Ukulele tuning: gCEA

STEPHEN C. FOSTER

OLD DOG TRAY

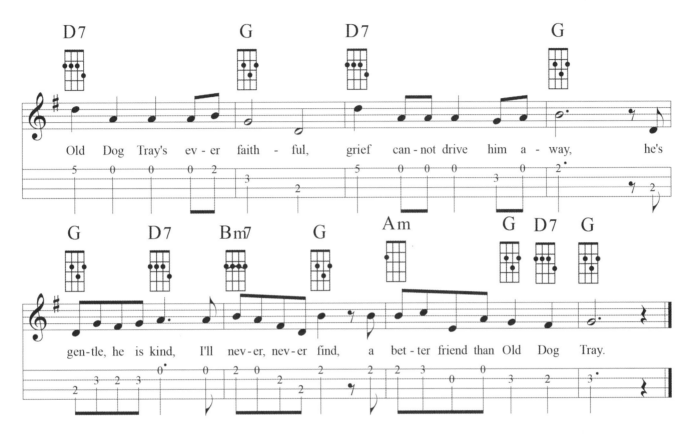

Old Dog Tray's ev-er faith-ful, grief can-not drive him a-way, he's gen-tle, he is kind, I'll nev-er, nev-er find, a bet-ter friend than Old Dog Tray.

2. The forms I called my own
    have vanished one by one,
The loved ones, the dear ones,
    have all passed away,
Their happy smiles have flown,
    their gentle voice gone;
I've nothing left but Old Dog Tray.
CHORUS

3. When tho'ts recall the past,
    his eyes are on me cast;
I know that he feels
    what my breaking heart would say;
Al'tho he cannot speak,
    I'll vainly, vainly seek,
A better friend than Old Dog Tray.
CHORUS

AT RIGHT:
American Bloodhound

OLD FOLKS AT HOME

Ukulele tuning: gCEA

STEPHEN C. FOSTER

OLD FOLKS AT HOME

2. All roun' the little farm I wandered,
    when I was young;
Then many happy days I squandered,
    many the songs I sung.
When I was playing with my brother,
    happy was I;
Oh! Take me to my kind old mother,
    There let me live and die.
REFRAIN

2. One little hut among the bushes,
    one that I love,
Still sadly to my mem'ry rushes,
    no matter where I rove.
When will I see the bees a-humming,
    all roun' the comb?
When will I hear the banjo strumming,
    down in my good old home?
REFRAIN

Ring The Banjo

Ukulele tuning: gCEA

Stephen C. Foster

RING THE BANJO

Chorus: Ring, Ring the ban-jo! I like that good old song, come a-gain my true love, — Oh! where you been so long?

2. Oh! Never count the bubbles
    while there's water in the spring.
   The field hand has no troubles
    while he's got this song to sing.
   The beauties of creation
    will never lose their charm,
   While I roam the old plantation
    with my true love on my arm.
   CHORUS

3. Once I was so lucky,
    my massa set me free,
   I went to old Kentucky
    to see what I could see.
   I could not go no farther,
    I turn to massa's door,
   I love him all the harder,
    I'll go away no more.
   CHORUS

4. Early in the morning
    of a lovely summer day,
   My massa send me warning
    he like to hear me play.
   On the banjo tapping,
    I come with dulcet strain;
   Old massa fall a-napping,
    he'll never wake again.
   CHORUS

5. My love I'll have to leave you
    while the river's running high;
   But I ne'er can deceive you,
    so don't you wipe your eye.
   I'm goin' to make some money;
    but I'll come another day,
   I'll come again, my honey,
    if I have to work my way.
   CHORUS

UNCLE NED

Ukulele tuning: gCEA

STEPHEN C. FOSTER

There was an old field hand and his name was Un-cle Ned, he's dead long a-go, long a - go; He had no wool on the top of his head, the place where the wool ought to grow. Then

Chorus: lay down the shov - el and the hoe,_____ hang up the fid - dle and the bow; no more hard work for poor Old Ned, he is gone where the good field hands go.

UNCLE NED

2. His fingers were long like the cane in the brake,
      He had no eyes for to see,
    He had no teeth for to eat the corn cake
      So he had to let the corn cake be.
    CHORUS

The first time I heard this song was on a recording by balladeer, Burl Ives, who in my estimation was one of the greatest of American folk singers. I had the opportunity to interview him briefly when he was appearing as "Big Daddy" in the Broadway show "Cat on a Hot Tin Roof." Asked what his favorite folk song was, he replied that it was the one most recently learned. He expressed regrets that he was not a better guitarist. This was surprising since the strength and beauty of his performance was in its unvarnished accompaniment. But having said this, Burl Ives was still a very accomplished guitarist, his style perfect for the ballads he brought to life.

Unfortunately, Burl's recording in later years lost the touch of his pure folk singing. They became commercial with orchestral arrangements to the exclusion of his guitar alone.

There's a monument to Stephen Foster and his song "Uncle Ned" on the campus of the University of Pittsburgh. Sculptured in 1900 by Giuseppe Moretti, it depicts Foster seated with pen in hand while below him sits a barefoot banjo player representing the many banjo references in Foster's songs.

We are Coming, Father Abraham
300,000 More

From a poem by
JAMES SLOANE GIBBONS

STEPHEN C. FOSTER

WE ARE COMING, FATHER ABRAHAM, 300,000 MORE

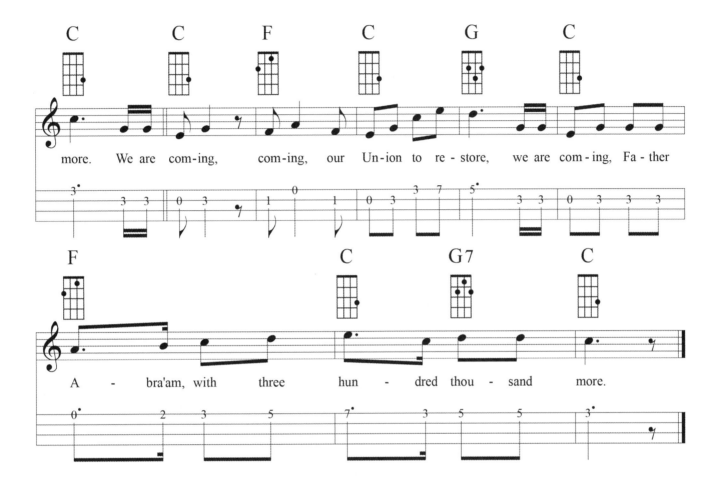

more. We are com-ing, com-ing, our Un-ion to re-store, we are com-ing, Fa-ther

A - bra'am, with three hun - dred thou - sand more.

The stirring lyrics of this song were from a poem written in 1862 by James Sloan Gibbons, a Northern Abolitionist, in response to Abraham Lincoln's call for 300,000 volunteers to fight for the Union Army. So popular was the poem that it was set to music by eight different composers. For a different version by composer Luther Orlando Emerson, see *Centerstream's "Songs of the Civil War for Ukulele."*

AT RIGHT:
Tintype of Black Union Soldier

ABOUT THE AUTHOR

Dick Sheridan first heard the beautiful songs of Stephen Foster when he was a very young child being brought up in a musical household. Both his parents played piano and the family's music cabinet was filled with songbooks that always included at least one of Foster's memorable songs. Those songs became as familiar as the popular tunes of the day, sung in music classes, at community sing-alongs, and at every family gathering around the parlor piano or phonograph.

Dick's urge to play these songs himself led to efforts that began in grade school years. He vividly recalls sitting on the front porch steps of his childhood home trying to fit the notes of "Oh! Susanna" and "Camptown Races" to a small Hohner diatonic harmonica. When a soprano uke was given to him one Christmas, a new door was opened and he found he could now sing and accompany himself with ukulele chords. Later came a harmonica holder, and Dick became a one-man band with a Foster song always on the top of the playlist.

Through the progression of instruments that Dick learned to play – uke, guitar, autoharp, mandolin, banjo – the fondness of songs by Stephen Foster remained constant with new zest added whenever a previously unknown song was discovered, researched, and put into to the repertoire. "Old Dog Tray"

and "Nelly Was A Lady" were just such songs, now numbered among the favorites.

Dick fondly remembers that in his young years there were church groups and fraternal organizations that presented revival minstrel shows with silver-throated tenors vocalizing "Beautiful Dreamer" and choruses of energetic performers singing "Camptown Races" while beating time on their elbows, thighs, and kneecaps with quivering tambourines. Sadly, because of negative connotations of some early minstrelsy, the minstrel show has faded from popularity. Once in adult years while searching for props for a fun-themed business meeting, Dick found racks and racks of minstrel attire in a costume shop – sequined tuxedoes, spangled dresses, multi-colored top hats – all forgotten and neglected.

The minstrel show may have faded from popularity but not the songs of Stephen Foster that were such a vital part of them. Foster's songs continue to be played, delighting singers, musicians, and audiences much as they did well over a hundred years ago. As a case in point, Dick points out that even his Dixieland jazz band, which he leads and plays banjo with, is ever ready to pull out a Foster tune, often by request, and always to the delight of enthusiastic listeners.